LOOK

I WROTE A

Book

By Jan Mendoza

Look, I Wrote a Book   ©2020   Jan Mendoza

ISBN
9780982605066
Revised March 2023

Far West Publishing

This book makes references to trademarks for editorial purposes only; the author makes no commercial claims on their use. Nothing contained herein is intended to express judgement on or affect the validity of the legal status of any term or word as a trademark, service mark or other proprietary mark.

Disclaimer

Contents of this book are solely based on the opinions and experiences of the author. Results from the advice and opinions of this book may vary. Content of this book is informational only and is not to be construed as legal or professional advice. Information contained herein is a general guideline only. Author accepts no liability or responsibility for any loss or damages caused, or thought to be caused, by following the advice or recommendations in this book. While author made every attempt to ensure that the information in this book is accurate and up to date, mistakes or inaccuracies may well exist. It is up to the reader to research all aspects of book publishing,on their own, to be very well educated on the subject and to not use this book as their only resource.

www.janmendoza.com

@janmendoza1 (Twitter)

Manufactured in the United States of America.

Table of Contents

Introduction

When I set out to write my first book, I thought, "What could be so hard about this?" I had written some pretty good short stories in college, and I spent a good portion of my life writing for a living. Words are kind of my "thing." However, writing a book was another story. I had never done that before! How was I going to get it published? Was getting a "book deal" with a big publisher out of the question? Was self-publishing a better option? I had so many questions, and before I put one word down on paper, I started to do the other thing I was good at: research.

Google became my best friend, and I read every blog, book, and article I could find. I watched YouTube videos, and I attended workshops and lectures about writing and publishing. After hearing the never-ending horror stories of how impossible it is to get a traditional book deal and the years it would take to see my work in print, I decided to self-publish my books. I found a way to self-publish and get my books listed for sale on the big retail websites. I found a shining light and went for it. However, I quickly learned that just because I have a book on Amazon, people are not going to automatically find it. I needed a web presence, a blog, a marketing platform, social media followers, a good editor, a nice package, a good cover, an ebook version, a book trailer, a press release, and much more. And.. drum roll please my book STILL may not be read!

So, after a few months and a huge notebook full of information, along with many websites and blogs bookmarked, I set off on my journey of book writing and publishing. After my books were up on Amazon, people started asking me how to get their books published. I would say GOOGLE IT, that's what I did! Then they'd say, "But I just want to write a book. Can't you just tell me?" Well, my friends, here I am "telling you." This is just a short version of how I navigated the winding road of writing and publishing books. In this guide, I will give you some basic information on getting your book published by a big publishing company, but since I personally didn't go that route, all I can tell you is what I found in my research. My research concluded that getting a big book deal is like playing the lottery. Your chances are one in a million. Personally, I wasn't willing to wait five years to see my book published. Life is too short, and anything could happen. I wanted my books out in the world while I was still alive! Whatever path you decide to take when publishing your book, you might find your ride a little different than mine. I just hope this little book will give you the head-start and the push you need. Just make sure to buckle your seat-belt because the ride is about to get bumpy!

CHAPTER 1
Be an Author! Write a Book!

Write a book, get it published, and become famous! This is the dream of many authors. Who wouldn't want fame and fortune? I'll settle for having my book in print or on an e-reader and hope that a few people read it. What I discovered in my journey as an author is that writing is a great way to relieve stress, get rid of emotional baggage, and is a wonderful form of meditation. I love to write.

Do you have a novel, a memoir, a children's book, or a book of poems that has been floating around in your head for ages? I have one thing to say to you. WRITE YOUR BOOK! You won't regret it!

I know you have questions—big ones! How will I get my book printed? How much does it cost? How do I find a publisher? How long does it take to write a book and get it published? As these are all very important questions, don't worry about these issues just yet. Worrying about the nuts and bolts of publishing in this stage of the game will only clutter your brain with unnecessary blocks. At this point, just concentrate on writing your book and being the best writer you can be.

Your book is your legacy. Even if you are only writing for your family, you are leaving a piece of yourself behind for future generations to read. I think everyone should write a book. Once you start writing, you will be surprised at how easily the words flow! Maybe you have yummy recipes that you have created over the years with stories to go with them. Make a book! This is your gift to your family and the world!

Millions of books are published each year in the United States. The competition is beyond fierce. However, don't let this dismal statistic keep you from writing a book. We all have something to share, so share it! I hope to help you get started on your journey as an author!

Step 1
Read Books

Read books just like the ones you want to write. Before I wrote my memoir, Fire Girl, I read several memoirs by female firefighters. I wanted to see how these authors told their stories. I wanted to find out how they dealt with writing about real people. I found that authors vary in the way they tell stories. I quickly discovered which stories were easy to read and understand. Reading helps you discover different styles of writing, so if you want to be an author, you must read!

Step 2
Write an Outline

Don't worry about formatting your book with the correct margins for print at this stage. All of this is done at the very end, when your finished, polished manuscript is ready for print. Then, you or your publisher will format your book. You can't know where to place your margins if you don't know how thick your book will be.

If you have a storyline or a series of topics in mind, write down a list of chapters. At this point, you don't need a final determination of chapter names. You can change them later. An outline of your book is a great jumping-off point when you are looking at a blank screen. Under your outline headings or chapter names, list topics or story lines as you think of them. Most beginning authors need this sort of structure to keep them on task. Some authors don't like being so rigid and may have the skill to keep their stories organized in their brains. This is all up to the individual. Writing an outline helped me tremendously! Now that you have your outline, start writing your book! I use Microsoft Word to write my initial working manuscript. This is the software that most editors use. When you are working with an editor, you both will be able to track the changes made to your manuscript using this software. Again, don't get all caught up in the formatting until the very end. I know you are itching to make your headings look nice and your paragraphs all nicely indented.

Step 3
Hire an Editor

Whether you submit your work to a big publisher or are self-published, you want your work to be in the best shape possible. Editors can help you with the development of your story, plot structure, character development, voice, pacing, scene structure, dialogue, factual errors, over-use of passive language, consistency, repetitiveness, gaps, clumsy writing, incorrect grammar usage, incorrect punctuation, and spelling. To have your book fully polished, you will need more than a proofreader looking for spelling errors.

You may need to hire a couple of different editors who specialize in different things on that list. But if you are limited in funds, at least use a site like www.quillbot.com/grammar-check. You can cut and paste your chapters into the site, and it's pretty good at finding most grammar errors. It's free to use, but if you want more robust editing that helps with complex sentences, etc., there is a monthly subscription. It might be worth it to purchase it while writing your book.

Ask the prospective editor if they have examples of books they have edited. Professional editors will edit sample pages of your book for free. You can see how they work and if you like them personally. You will be working with this person for a while, so make sure you aren't dealing with someone grouchy that you don't like! Also, make sure you both agree on the terms. How many revisions can you make? Can you bail out of the contract if you aren't working well together? All of these things will need to be spelled out at the beginning. Don't be hurt when you get your draft sent back with all sorts of corrections and suggestions. Your awesome book depends on a great editor! As you go through the editing process, read your book out loud. This helps in finding grammatical or spelling errors. Speaking the words out loud will help you find sentences that either run on too long or make no sense whatsoever. After your manuscript is fully written and edited, let it sit for a week or two. Then read it again with fresh eyes.

PROTECTING YOUR "ASS"-ETS

When writing my memoir about being one of the first female firefighters for the California Department of Forestry, I had to make sure that my claim to this statement was correct and undeniable. I needed to receive written confirmation of my claim from the State of California, which required several public records requests from various state agencies. The next thing I did was change the names of the real-life people in my book to protect their identities. However, changing names may not completely protect identities if you are describing a particular place and time.

Writing about other people in your memoir may make you a little nervous, especially if some of your stories about them are unflattering. Defamation of character is a sticky wicket and could get you in all sorts of legal trouble. If your book is nonfiction, be absolutely sure that what you are saying in it is true. Do some research on this subject or get legal advice from a lawyer who specializes in these sorts of issues.

Janette Walls wrote a book about her grandmother called Half Broke Horses. Since her grandmother has long been dead, and she only had stories that were most likely true but unverifiable, Walls decided to write her story as a true-life novel! A novel is fiction, in case you didn't know. Because she labeled her book fiction, liabilities and hurt feelings were greatly diminished.

What NOT to do:

James Frey wrote a book called A Million Little Pieces. This book was published by a big publisher, touted by Oprah Winfrey and labeled as a non-fiction memoir. It came to light that a lot of his story was completely made-up. He got in hot water for this deceitfulness. If he had labeled his book fiction he might have been protected from scrutiny. However, he may have had a more difficult time getting a book deal going that route. Don't label your book non-fiction if it can be challenged as not being true. This will come back to bite you BIG TIME!

LET IT FLY!

Our books are an extension of ourselves, so we want them to be the best they possibly can be. However, since we strive for perfection, we have a tendency to hang on to them for much too long. We fix, we overcorrect, we change, and we go back to the way it was in the beginning. I know authors who take years to write their manuscript before it gets a first look by an editor because they keep re-writing their book! Don't fall into this endless loop. Get your manuscript to an editor and let him/her help you decide what needs changing, deleting, or adding. Life is short, and it can change in an instant! Get your book out there!

Let that baby bird fly from the nest!

Now you need to make some decisions on how you will get your edited and polished manuscript into the hands of the public! Will you self-publish? Will you look for an agent? The next chapters will hopefully help you decide which road you will travel.

CHAPTER 2
Traditional Publishing

As I stated in the beginning, millions of books are published each year. Don't let this stop you from living your dreams. If you have the dream of being signed by a big publisher, then by all means, go for it. Beware; this is going to be a difficult and lengthy process. Are you ready? Hang on, here we go!

Roadblock #1

Large publishing companies such as Penguin Random House, Simon & Schuster, and Harper Collins hardly ever read manuscripts from unknown authors. Here is a direct quote from the Simon & Schuster website (simonandschuster.com). "Simon & Schuster does not review, retain, or return unsolicited materials or artwork. We suggest that prospective authors and illustrators submit their manuscripts through a professional literary agent."

What is a literary agent? A reputable literary agent spends years gaining the trust of book publishing companies. Most agents made their connections by working for big publishing companies in the past. Literary agents know the business of books inside and out and will negotiate your book deal with your business interests in mind first and foremost.

Roadblock #2

Finding an agent who has connections with big publishers is a difficult task! It really helps to know someone who personally knows an agent. If you can get a personal referral, you stand a better chance of getting your query letter read. You first need to find the right agent for your book. You don't want to send your memoir to an agent who deals mostly with fiction or cookbooks. You also don't want to waste your time sending your material to an agent who is already representing someone with a book exactly like yours. That's a conflict of interest.

So, how do you find an agent? If you don't already have a personal connection with an agent, you will have to do a ton of research. Take a look at the acknowledgement page in the back of your favorite book. A lot of times, the author will thank their agent. Is that book a romance novel? Do you have a romance novel, but of a different sort? Write down the name of that agent. Now, go to the library, bookstores, and even yard sales to look for books, with a special thanks to an agent, editor, or publisher. You will eventually have quite a list of potential contacts. There are also online directories that list agents. I have some listed in the back of this book. Now that you have your list, go online to see if they have a website where you can get more information. Getting an agent can take months—maybe years. I've heard stories where authors sent their query letters to 50 or more agents only to hear back from just a handful with rejection letters. However, the rejection letters gave some hints as to how the authors could improve their books.

Agents receive thousands of manuscripts a week. Most of the time, they have an assistant reading their mail. Your query letter and proposal could end up in a pile, never to be read. However, agents do keep their eyes out for self-published authors who are gaining in popularity. If you are having trouble getting the attention of an agent, or you just don't want to go through all of the hassle and heartache, you may want to head down the road and knock on the door of a smaller publishing company. Smaller publishing companies typically don't work with agents.

Small Publishing Companies

There are midsize to small publishing companies that will take unsolicited material without an agent. Small publishing companies will state on their website what type of manuscripts they are looking for with their submission guidelines. Some publishers only want poetry, while others want science fiction. Don't waste your time sending your manuscript to a publisher that isn't looking for your type of book! Some small publishers charge a submission or reading fee. I wouldn't do this unless you truly believed in this particular publisher. If you are paying a bunch of publishers to read your material, the cost can start to add up. Look for publishers who are taking submissions for free. Also note that an agent should NEVER charge a reading fee.

Some small publishing companies hold contests and charge an entry fee. Again, be careful, as you don't want to spend a ton of money for the "chance" that your manuscript will be accepted. Do your research and see what other books are being published by these small companies. Amazon sales rankings are a good way to find out if a small publisher is good at marketing authors.

Steps to Traditional Publishing (The Long Road)

Step 1

Draft a query letter and proposal. This is your introduction and sales pitch to either an agent or a book publishing company, stating why your book is marketable or unique, that you have a marketing platform or following, and that your book has the potential to make them a profit. You will need to do your own marketing research to see if your book has any direct competition. Your marketing research data will need to be included in your proposal. Include sample chapters of your polished and professionally edited manuscript. Go online and look at sample query letters and proposals. Some agents and publishing companies will have specific guidelines as to what needs to be in your proposal. You may want to hire a professional who knows how to put together a book proposal. Your proposal must be PERFECT!

NOTE: As stated earlier, most publishing companies and agents will NOT accept unsolicited material. Meaning you need a major connection with the publishing company for your proposal to NOT immediately end up in the garbage. Sometimes, publishing companies have rare opportunities for unsolicited material. Do a Google search for "publishers or agents that are accepting unsolicited material."

Step 2

You have found a literary agent! CONGRATULATIONS! I hope you're still in good health after your long wait! Your agent will now start to pitch your material to publishing companies. However, I have more disheartening news. Publishing companies only accept a limited amount of material from agents per year. It can take your agent months to get a publishing company to consider your book. It can take another year after that to finally see your book in print.

Step 3

Look for small publishing companies that are taking unsolicited material from authors.

Pros of traditional publishing:

You might get an advance payment while you are still writing your book. (This is not guaranteed to new authors.)

The publisher will do all of the work, such as development, formatting, editing, and printing. Your book will be distributed to major book retail outlets, both online and in walk-in physical stores. Your book will be submitted to libraries, and you will be listed in the Library of Congress.

The publisher will do the marketing. You may get press in major news outlets if they market you properly. However, some authors still have to do a lot of their own marketing if the publishing company is small.

Cons of Traditional Publishing

You will lose control of your content. The publisher makes all the decisions as to what goes in and what stays out!

You don't own the publishing rights to your book. You can't just decide one day to go with another publisher. Get legal advice before you sign your book rights away!

You will have to negotiate a royalty, which might be small if you are a new and unknown author.

If your book doesn't sell, the publisher will drop you like a hot rock!

It can take years to see your book in print—this includes the months or years it took to find an agent and/or publisher after receiving hundreds of rejection letters!

CHAPTER 3

Self-Publishing - The Indie-Author Approach

The Indie-Author ApproachSelf-published Author Inks Seven-Figure Deal With Penguin

This is an actual headline! Check out these success stories of indie authors!

In 1931, the author of The Joy of Cooking self-published and paid a local printing company to print 3000 copies. Later, Bobbs-Merrill Company acquired the rights. This book has since sold over 18 million copies.

The contemporary trilogy Fifty Shades of Grey by E.L. James was originally published online as Twilight fan fiction before the author decided to self-publish. This book was not only picked up by a major publishing company; it was made into a movie.

Tracy Garvis Graves was rejected by dozens of agents and publishing companies. She did the "unthinkable" and self-published her ebook called On the Island. She slowly gained popularity, and eventually Graves was noticed by the big publishers, including Amazon, HarperCollins, and Penguin. A movie deal is also in the works.

Author Andy Weir self-published his book, The Martian. It was such a success that it was picked up by Crown Publishing in 2014 and then made into a movie.

Amanda Brown self-published her book, "Legally Blonde!" It was turned into a movie with a sequel starring Reese Witherspoon.

Print on Demand In the early 2000s, a publishing platform called digital Print-On-Demand technology (POD) hit the streets. This is a printing technology and business process in which a book is not printed until an order has been received, allowing books to be printed in small quantities. Back in the old days, self-publishers had to pay a few thousand dollars to have their manuscript manufactured by an offset printing company. The author was then required to order a minimum quantity of 1,000 or more copies. The self-published author had to store these books in their garage and mail them out to customers. With POD manufacturing, once a customer orders a book online, that one book is printed and mailed by the POD manufacturer directly to the customer.

Amazon and a host of other companies are now able to publish small indie authors using POD technology. The beautiful thing is there are no up-front costs to you or the publishing company for printing. Once you upload your finished manuscript to one of these companies, your book is now available for sale at a multitude of places.

Here is how Amazon explains it:

www.kdp.amazon.com:"Booksellers and libraries purchase paperbacks from large distributors. If you enroll your paperback in Expanded Distribution, we'll make your book available to distributors so booksellers and libraries can find your book and order it.We currently work with US distributors, but booksellers and libraries outside of the US may purchase books from these US distributors. It's free to enroll your paperback in Expanded Distribution, and it allows your book to be made broadly available outside of Amazon. nrolling your paperback in Expanded Distribution doesn't guarantee it will be accepted by distributors or ordered by a particular bookseller or library. The decision to list your book lies with distributors and the decision to order your book lies solely with the individual booksellers and libraries. We can't

provide details on which booksellers and libraries purchased your book."
https://kdp.amazon.com/en_US/help/topic/GQTT4W3T5 AYK7L45

A Word on Brick and Mortar Retail Bookstores

Even though your book is listed in the Ingram catalog, where brick and mortar book stores can order and stock your books, don't count on seeing it at one of these any time soon. Big-box retail book stores typically order from traditional publishing companies. Book stores have limited space on their shelves, and they only want to stock books they absolutely know will sell. The big publishing companies have large marketing teams that sell books to bookstores. You are competing with these giant companies for shelf space. Small independent book stores may stock self-published books, but you would have to purchase your own books at wholesale, mark them up a dollar or two, and sell them to the bookstore owner. The bookstore has to make a profit, so you won't make much from your book this way. However, you could have a book signing and bring in all of your friends. This is good business for the bookstore and a great sales pitch for them to stock your books! It's important to note that if your books don't sell, the bookstore will ship the unsold books back, and you will have to send them a refund. More often than not, the book will have been handled by shoppers and will be damaged. You will then be stuck with used, bent books. As you can see, bookstores expect you to give them a huge discount! You will have to sell a lot of books in a bookstore to make any sort of profit.

Publishers that charge a feeCompanies that charge authors to publish books are sometimes called "vanity publishers." However, I have found that these publishers vary in what they offer and the rights and control you may lose. Some of these publishers charge the author between $600.00 and $15,000.00, to publish your book. They will be the publisher on record, and will hold all of the rights to your book. These companies take your manuscript and do the editing, formatting, printing, and, occasionally, marketing. Sometimes they make you feel very "special" by having you submit your manuscript for their "acceptance." You will be paid a royalty from sales, but I've heard that some don't pay the author anything at all. Why an author would sign up with the latter is beyond me!

I have found that there are other self-publishing companies that charge a fee to do some or all of the heavy lifting for you, such as editing, formatting, printing, marketing, and other services. You can purchase a la carte or a package of services. These companies will let you be the publisher on record and will submit your book for distribution. Make sure you are in full control of your book and rights before you pay any publisher to perform any extra services.

CHAPTER 4
Ready Your Print Book For Sale

When self-publishing, you will need to decide on the trim size (width and height) of your book. You will then format the interior of your book to fit within the parameters of the size that you chose. You will create a front and back cover, obtain an ISBN, and decide the name of your imprint (the name of your publishing company). I will go over each of these phases. First, let's talk about the size.

Trim Size for Paperback Books

In the book publishing world, the actual dimensions of the book are called the trim size. This is NOT the thickness of your book. Below are the trim sizes you will get to choose from in KDP.Amazon that are considered standards for the paperback industry. I have bolded the commonly used trim sizes for most paperback books.

5 x 8 inches, 12.7 x 20.32 centimeters
5.25 x 8 inches, 13.335 x 20.32 centimeters
5.5 x 8.5 inches, 13.97 x 21.59 centimeters - Most commonly used for many types of books
5.06 x 7.81 inches, 12.84 x 19.84 centimeters
6 x 9 inches, 15.24 x 22.86 centimeters - Most commonly used for many types of books
6.14 x 9.21 inches, 15.6 x 23.4 centimeters
6.69 x 9.61 inches, 17 x 24.4 centimeters
7 x 10 inches, 17.78 x 25.4 centimeters
7.44 x 9.69 inches, 18.9 x 24.6 centimeters
7.5 x 9.25 inches, 19.1 x 23.5 centimeters

8 x 10 inches, 20.32 x 25.4 centimeters - Most commonly used for children's book
8.5 x 11 inches, 21.59 x 27.94 centimeters - Most commonly used for children's book

Once you have determined the trim size for your book, it's now time to format your fully edited and ready-for-print manuscript. You can try to tackle this yourself or ship your work off to a person who has expertise in formatting a print book. I formatted all of my books myself by using desktop publishing software called PagePlus by Sarif. This software not only does a great job formatting books; it's also a fantastic tool for creating cover designs and editing images. I find it user-friendly and intuitive, even if you haven't used desktop publishing programs in the past. Many people format their books with Microsoft Word or the free version called Open Office. KDP.Amazon has a great free MS Word template that you can download. This template is completely formatted, and all you need to do is insert the body of your book. Just choose the trim size of your book and download that particular template. Here is the link.

https://kdp.amazon.com/en_US/help/topic/G201834230

If you research the topic of book formatting software, you will find everyone has their favorite, and there are many out there to choose from. If your book is mostly words, MS Word or something similar should suit you just fine. If your book is heavy with graphics and illustrations, you might find Page Plus or another type of desktop publishing software is better.

Fonts

Times New Roman, Book Antiqua, Palatino, and Calibri are common fonts that are used in books. I'm using Book Antiqua (12 pts) for this particular book. You will want to keep your font size between 10 and 12 pts. If you are writing a children's book, the font size may be larger, maybe around 14 pts.

Margins

When setting up your document, make sure you click "mirrored margins." This will make your facing pages the same, but mirrored. The margin will be wider in the middle of the book. This is called the "gutter margin." Here is how I set up the margins for my book Fire Girl, which is a 6 x 9 book with 139 pages.

Inside: 0.88	Outside: 0.5
Top: 0.75	bottom: 0.75

The gutter margin settings are dependent on the thickness of your book. If you have a very thick book with lots of pages, your gutter margins will be wider. Your self publishing company will state on its website the recommended margin settings.

Paragraphs

Notice how the sentences in print books all line up on the right side? This is called "justified." Justified paragraphs make for a cleaner looking book. However, a lot of your words may be hyphenated, and some of your words may have more spaces between them than you like. You will need to adjust your settings in your publishing software for how many minimum letters a word is allowed to be hyphenated.

Also, the spaces between your letters and words will need to be adjusted. You may have to do some of these things manually, as your software may not pick up everything even after you adjust the settings. These are the little things you will have to go over in great detail when you are formatting. You will need to make little adjustments here and there to make your document as tidy as possible.

Chapter Headings and Page Numbers

Your chapter headings can have names, or you can simply number them, or do both! This is completely up to you. Page numbers typically start with Chapter One being the first page. Everything before that is called front matter. You will need to set which page is actually printed ("Page 1") when formatting your book. Front matter will have no page numbers.Make your chapter headings large and/or bold. You may even use a fancier font if you like. Some authors like to put a little graphic in their chapter heading.

Front Matter

The front matter is everything that comes before your first chapter. Front matter is your title page, copyright page, dedication page, table of contents, introduction, foreword, and/or prologue. The one page you MUST have in your front matter is the copyright page listing your ISBN. (More on the ISBN later.) The copyright page is mandatory if you want your book published. Look at the copyright page of this book. Notice where I have the title, the ISBN and other legal disclaimers. To protect yourself, include a disclaimer that you will not be held liable if someone claims they were harmed by reading your book. Also include your copyright language. On this page, include the name of your publishing company, your Library of Congress control number, and your website address. Take a look at a professionally published book. Study how the pages of the front matter are put together. You will notice that there are blank pages separating some of the segments of the front matter. Some books may have a foreword written by a friend, an introduction to the book, or a prologue to the story about to be told. Some books with many chapters will have a table of contents. This is a great feature for the nonfiction book; where the reader may jump ahead to something special that you wrote about.

Body of Work

Now we are at the meat and potatoes of your book. Chapters typically begin on the right side pages of the book. When you are formatting, try to keep this in mind. If your chapter ends with just a very short paragraph at the top of the left page, insert a photo or a graphic to fill up the blank space. This is completely optional and something that I do.

Photos and Graphics

For memoirs or non-fiction, authors typically place a photo here and there throughout the book. However, the bulk of the photos are typically in the middle and encompass several pages. Since you are self-publishing, you can decide what photos or graphics you want to include. Be sure that all of your photos are print quality and at least 300 dpi. Remember, when you are converting your book for e-readers, your photos may not show up very well on some devices.

Get permission to use other people's photos, graphics, poems, song lyrics, and other works that may be protected by copyright! Don't rip images off the Internet; you will be sued for copyright infringement. If you need photos, go to a photo and image company such as ShutterStock.com or 123RF.com. You will find thousands of images, and the cost is typically

$5.00 to $10.00 per photo. With a standard license, you may use that photo in print up to 100,000 times. As a self-publisher, if you sell 100,000 books, you better be shopping for an agent to get you a great book deal! That's a lot of books!

The Back Matter

This is where you will place your epilogue, your acknowledgements, a bibliography, a list of resources and links, further reading, your bio, a sales pitch for your next book, or a word index. These pages are completely optional and are numbered.

Cover Art

Your book cover is the first thing someone sees, so make it a good one! Go online and look at the covers of some of the best-selling books. What kinds of fonts are used? How big are the letters? Do the letters go with the photo or graphic? What are the colors that catch your eye? Which cover screams READ ME?

Make your cover colorful with an eye-catching graphic or photo that really describes your book! Make a few different covers and get people to vote on them via social media.

Most self-publishing companies will have a template for designing your book cover. They also have easy-to-use online book cover generators. I happen to like the freedom of designing my own covers using Page Plus and the KDP.Amazon template that I download and place into my document. The template will tell you where the bar code will be placed and where the danger zones are so that your images and words won't be cut off during the printing process.

Ready for Upload

Now that your book and cover are completely formatted, it's time to convert your document into a PDF. You will have two PDF documents: one for your entire book interior and one for your cover. Your self-publishing company will tell you exactly what settings to use when converting your document into a PDF.

CHAPTER 5
ISBN - The Identifier

ISBN stands for the International Standard Book Number. This is the number that identifies a particular book to the world. If you plan to sell your book in bookstores, libraries, or through online retailers like Amazon.com, you must have an ISBN.

The ISBN identifies the following:
Title/subtitle
Author
Page Count
Format (paperback, hardcover, audiobook, ebook)
Trim Size
Publisher
Edition

A new ISBN has to be assigned to your book if any of these items vary. For example, if you have paperback, hardcover, and ebook versions of your book, you will need three different ISBNs. Bowker is the official company that issues these numbers. Bowker also maintains Books in Print®, which is the leading bibliographic database for publishers, retailers, and libraries around the world. You can purchase one ISBN for $125.00 or a block of ten ISBNs for $295.00. Since you may have different versions of your book, it's more cost-effective to buy the block of ten. You own these ISBNs forever, and you don't have to assign them to a book until you are ready. Buying your own ISBNs directly from Bowker allows you to submit your work anywhere you like to multiple self-publishing companies.

KDP.Amazon give you a free ISBN and will be listed as your publisher. However, you can only list your book with them and no one else. They will still list your book for expanded distribution as described earlier, including libraries and academic institutions. Unfortunately, you can't submit your book to another self-publishing company when using the free KDP.Amazon ISBN. You will still own your book and retain all rights. There have been very successful self-publishers who used the free ISBN from KDP.Amazon

Barcodes

The bar code is a representation of the ISBN in a form that can be identified by scanners. The bar code might also have other information embedded in it, such as the price of the book and the type of currency. The publishing company that you work with will give you a barcode for free and place it on the back cover of your book using the ISBN that you choose. If you are using their cover design template, they will have a place for the barcode. Bowkers sells barcodes, but you don't need to purchase any. Your self-publishing company will give you one for free.

Your Imprint

If you decided to purchase your own ISBNs directly from Bowker, you can now list your own imprint (publishing company) on your books. My imprint is Far West Publishing. You can name your publishing company anything you like. It's not absolutely necessary to have your own imprint, i.e., publishing company, but I think it looks professional and doesn't scream SELF-PUBLISHED to the world. (I just outed myself.) It's a great thing if you purchased a block of ISBNs because you have many books you want to share with the world. I purchased a block of ten. Also, you can go to Bowkerlink.com to officially register your publishing company with Bowker. All of your books will be listed in the Bowker Books print catalog under your publishing company name. This is pretty cool, but completely unnecessary if you only want to publish one book in your entire lifetime.

CHAPTER 6
Submit for Sale

Checklist

Your book has been professionally edited.
It has been formatted and triple-checked for errors, odd spacing, correct page numbers, etc.
You have created an awesome front and back cover.
You have your PDFs ready to submit and have followed all of the publishing company's PDF conversion instructions.

NOW IT GETS EXCITING!

When choosing a self-publishing company, you will have a few options. I have listed them in the resources section of this book. Each company will vary in the size and types of books they will print, and the royalty structure will also vary. My personal favorite is KDP.Amazon.com I found they have the highest royalty structure, and the majority of the population goes to Amazon to buy books. Based on my personal poll)

Since I publish with Amazon, I'll use them as the example from here on out. Sign up using your email address, click where it says "Start Title for Free," and follow the steps. They have a guided setup that I highly recommend.

As you go along in the set-up, you will add the ISBN for your book, set the sales price, and upload your interior and cover PDFs. Choose expanded distribution when prompted. Submit your bank information and your tax ID number (social security number). Amazon will be sending your royalty payments directly to your bank account, and you will get a 1099 at the end of the year if you live in the United States. When setting up your title, you will select the trim size of your book and decide if you want it in black and white or color. Color printing for the interior of your book is more expensive and will eat into your royalties, so keep that in mind. However, they will print your cover in color at no charge. You can choose a matte or glossy cover. They will also ask what color you want your pages to be: white or cream. I like cream; it's easy on the eyes and looks more professional. Also, you will be setting the page count of your book, including the blank ones. The higher the page count, the more it's going to cost to print. Your page count will dictate what your royalty will be. At this stage, you can click on the button "estimate your book's manufacturing cost." As of this writing, the manufacturing cost of a paperback book with 350 pages is about $5.05 USD per book. You can go to the calculator here: https://kdp.amazon.com/en_US/help/topic/G201834340 If you wanted to purchase 30 copies of your own book for an event, this is what you would pay per book plus shipping. If you sell your books at an event, you can mark up your book to a reasonable amount and keep the profit. I like to charge $10.00 per book at events. It's easy to make change!

KDP.Amazom.com also makes hardcover books. They are more expensive, so you will have to add a bigger markup. A hardback book is nice to have for display or if you want to give a signed hardback book to a friend or relative. I have hardback books listed for sale online, but they aren't big sellers. People would much rather spend 10 dollars for one of my paperbacks than 25 dollars for a hardcover.

Retail Pricing

When setting your price, decide what is affordable to your customers and what is still a decent royalty for you. The higher the retail price, the higher your royalty. Remember, your royalty will go down a bit if your book is sold by one of the other online bookstores with expanded distribution. Don't set your retail price so high that nobody buys your book! Keep it at a reasonable price!

The Final Touch

Once you upload your PDFs to the online publishing company that you've chosen, click the box that says "run automated print checks." The system will immediately let you know if you have any formatting issues, and you can preview your book online. The pages turn just like a real book. Common issues are incorrect margins or a photo that isn't 300 dpi. This checker will NOT catch spelling or grammar errors. Fix any errors that you deem legitimate. Sometimes, they will catch something that they think is an error but it actually isn't. If you see an error, fix your manuscript and re-upload your PDF. Check it again. If you think it all looks good, then order your proof at your wholesale price plus shipping. Getting your proof in the mail is really exciting. Read your proof carefully. Does the cover look good? Are the pages formatted to your liking? Now read your proof cover to cover as if you've never read it before. Have a friend read your proof and tell them to highlight any errors they see. Maybe there are too many periods after a sentence.. See what I just did there? Or, maybe you typed you instead of your. This is a common mistake, and editors aren't 100% perfect either. Put your proof away and wait a week before you read it again with fresh eyes! Read your proof out loud, as you did with your manuscript. You still have time to make little changes here and there. Just don't make BIG changes. Remember, let this bird FLY! You are just looking for obvious spelling, grammar, punctuation, and formatting errors at this point. When you think you are absolutely ready to publish, go back to your account dashboard and click PUBLISH!

Your book will be available on Amazon in a day or so (sometimes the same day), and it will start to populate on other bookstore websites in a week to two weeks - sometimes sooner.

CHAPTER 7
The World of Ebooks

Ebooks are books that can be read on a number of handheld devices. People read books on their e-readers, smart phones, tablets, laptops, and PCs. To make your book readable on these devices, it must be formatted in a word processing program in a particular way. Then the document is converted into a format suitable for e-readers. Epub seems to be the standard for most all e-readers. However, technology is always changing, so you may have to do a little research if you are reading this a year or more after publication.

It's a very smart move to have your book converted into an e-book. Since there isn't any printing involved, a customer buys your book, loads it onto their reader, and they are instantly reading your book. The sale price of your e-book will be much lower than that of your printed book.

Getting your book in an e-reader format is a little tricky. You must be familiar with Microsoft Word or an equivalent program. If you aren't a tech wiz, you may want to hire someone to convert the PDF version of your book to be ready for e-readers, especially if you have all sorts of tables, graphs, images, etc.

Publishing your Ebook

Kindle Direct (KDP -Amazon) is the biggest seller of e-books. However, Smashwords.com is the largest publisher among all the other ebook retailers (Barnes & Noble, Kobo, Lulu, Apple, and many others). Format your e-book so that you can submit it to both Kindle and Smashwords.

Amazon KDP "Select" Program

Amazon also has a program called KDP Select. This is where you can only sell your e-book through the Amazon KDP

Select program. Amazon will now make your book available for all sorts of Amazon's promotional programs where you get paid. The downside is that you may miss out on sales from other sources. BEWARE: Once you enroll in the Select program, you can't sell your eBook via your website, Smashwords or any other e-book service. You may want to enroll in the KDP Select program for a while and see how it goes. You can always cancel the KDP Select program and revert to the regular KDP Kindle program. You can then sell your eBook on other platforms such as Nook, Apple, etc. KDP Select is only for e-books and will not affect your print books. You can continue to sell your print books however you like. Do some research; there are many blog posts about KDP Select. The experience varies with different authors.

When you upload your e-book for Kindle and Smashwords, you will need to put in all of your financial information, such as your bank account number, social security number, or tax ID on their websites since these royalties are paid separately from your print books.

You will need to create a "cover" for your e-book. Since your e-book cover is going to be a much smaller version than what is on your print book, make sure it's very readable and eye-catching. There are many websites that teach you how to make the perfect ebook cover.

CHAPTER 8
Audiobooks

Audiobooks have become very popular in the past few years. ACX.com, owned by Amazon.com, is the place where you can hire a narrator and have your book come to life and be available on Audible.com, Amazon.com and iTunes. You can choose whether you want to pay your narrator a flat per-hour fee for the finished product, or you can choose a narrator who is willing to just share royalties, or both. Currently, I have a book that is being narrated, and I chose a narrator who is willing to take 100 dollars per finished hour and a split of my royalties. If you choose this route, you will get a polished-professional. So, if my book ends up being a three-hour audiobook, I'll pay her 300 dollars. It might take her longer to record, but I pay for the finished hours, not production hours. You must have worldwide copyright ownership of your book in order to have an audiobook for sale.

Once you list your manuscript on ACX.com and advertise your work for auditions with short chapter sections as audition scripts, you will get a host of narrators sending in samples for you to choose from. When you pick a narrator, you make them an offer. If they accept, they get to work recording and uploading your chapters to the site.

When choosing a narrator, make sure they have good audio quality. Listen for weird background noises, poor microphone quality, etc. I had to pass on a few good narrators because of their poor recording equipment.

CHAPTER 9
Marketing

Anyone can write a book, but not everyone's book will be read. With millions of books being published, it's pretty easy to get lost in all the noise! This is where you need to roll up your sleeves and get creative. Start your book's buzz about three months prior to its release. Even if you are published by a large publishing company, you will still need to promote yourself. Don't count on your publishing company to do all of your marketing, as they have many authors to manage. Some authors hire public relations firms or publicists to do their promotions. This can be quite expensive, so I am going to give you some ideas on how to do a lot of marketing on your own.

Marketing Platform

First, you must lay the foundation of your marketing plan. Here is the short list:

+Build a website—hire someone or build your own.

+Create a blog. Free platforms are wordpress.com or blogger.com.

+Social Media: If you are one of those social media hold-outs and don't know what Twitter, Facebook, Instagram, Pinterest, Tumblr, or LinkedIn are, you better learn! A good majority of your audience is on social media.

+Press Releases: Write a press release and send it out to your local news media: TV, radio, newspapers, and local organizational news letters. I did this and got booked to appear on local TV and radio morning shows.

+Speaking engagements at book stores, churches, schools, business organizations, homes, book fairs, conferences, and social gatherings of any sort Get out and talk about your book.

+Make videos and upload them on all of the social media sites. This is easily done with your phone! You can also make a book trailer if you are good at video editing.

+Enter contests. This can get pricey, as there are entry fees. Enter a couple and see how you do!

+Make business cards, fliers, brochures, bookmarks, or postcards of your book and hand them out to everyone you meet!

+Have a book launch event at the local library.

+Host a book launch event someplace fun, like a pub or a winery! This depends on your book or audience, of course.

+Place your book in your local gift or craft store, winery, etc. Let them know you are a local author. You'll have to give them a good wholesale rate and be willing to buy back any unsold books after a period of time.

+Let people pre-order your book. You can do this on Amazon.

+Start a newsletter and collect an email list. A newsletter keeps all of your friends and followers up-to-date on events, publication dates, etc. There are many ways to collect email addresses without being "spammy." Mailchimp.com is a great free newsletter service.

Your Blog

I found a few of my favorite authors by accidentally stumbling upon their blogs. One author I found blogged about her self-publishing adventure. She gave great advice on what to do and what NOT to do. She was so funny that I couldn't wait to read her actual books; two of which are memoirs that she self-published. Her blog became so popular that she now has a mystery novel that was picked up by a traditional publishing company.

So, what is a blog? It's a website where you write articles about interesting and fun things. There are blogs about hiking, raising kids, cooking, building stuff, and much more. If you are writing a memoir about your life in the music business, you may want to blog about the music industry in general. All the while, you are promoting your tell-all book. Maybe someone is searching the Internet for ways to get a record deal, and they stumble upon your blog! It happens! They go to your blog, love the information you are sharing, and notice that you wrote a book. They buy your book, love it, and tell all of their friends on social media about your blog and book. Perfect!

Get your readers interacting with your blog by asking them questions. For example, you could say, "I'm currently writing a science fiction novel! What is your favorite science fiction novel or movie and why?" "Who is your most favorite science fiction character and why?" Blog about some of the characters in your book and make up fun backstories for them aside from what you wrote in your book. Get your readers attached to your characters or stories.

Post the first chapter of your book on your blog for free to get people interested in reading the rest. Amazon will do this for you when your book is published; however, you can get a head start on your blog.

Write short stories or essays and post these on your blog, so your fans can get a sense of your writing style. You can also put these up on Kindle, so people can get to know you as a writer.

Hold a contest or drawing on your blog as you get closer to your publish date, with signed books as prizes. I had a drawing on my blog where I gave away a Starbucks gift card to people who subscribed. A little bribery goes a long way!

Be a guest blogger. This is called doing a "blog tour." There are bloggers out there who review books. Send them a free copy of your book for a review and get a guest spot on their blog.

Advertise your book for pre-sale on your blog and share your blog link on all of your other social media accounts.

Keep the Ball Rolling

Once your book is published, keep marketing it every chance you get—even years later! For example, if I see an article in the news about a subject similar to one of my books, I use that as an opportunity to mention my book when sharing the article!

A lot of people publish their book, do their big marketing campaign in the beginning, then get very lazy and stop talking about their book. They figure that their book is "old news" and not worth the effort of promoting it any longer. If you see your book sales drop, it's because you stopped marketing! As long as your book is out there, Promote! Promote! PROMOTE!

A good way to promote your book is to donate a portion of the proceeds to a good cause. This is a win-win! The organization that is benefiting from the proceeds will help promote your book! This not only helps great organizations with their fund-raising efforts, it helps your readers get to know you, especially if you have more than one book on the market! Also, you can write off your donations if the organization is a qualified non-profit. I give 100% of the Fire Girl proceeds to the Wildland Firefighter Foundation. It makes me happy to send them a check every month as well as read the wonderful reviews on Amazon.

Branding

If you were asked to do a radio interview about your book, how would you make it memorable to the listener? Writing a good tagline is a great way for people to remember what your book is about. Sometimes the title alone doesn't do the trick. Here are some taglines from books and movies:

Don't go in the water, Jaws

In Space, No One can Hear you Scream – Aliens

From Lost to Found on the Pacific Crest Trail – Wild

One Choice can Destroy You – Insurgent

Think of ways people will remember you and your book. Do you have a logo or a color scheme? Make these elements consistent on all of your marketing materials, website, blog, etc. All of these become your brand.

Book Reading Social Websites

People who are looking for books typically buy based on the review. Once your book is online, give copies to friends and family and beg (I mean encourage) them to write a review on Amazon or Goodreads.com.

Social media sites that are geared toward reading enthusiasts are extremely popular and a very important tool for authors. People share what they are reading, give recommendations, have discussion groups, and you can see what is sitting on their virtual book shelves. Goodreads.com seems to be the most popular, so make sure you have an author profile on this site. Goodreads has a fantastic author program where you can do a giveaway in exchange for reviews, which results in new readers! They also have a great author feedback group for you to join. You will get all sorts of valuable information on how to market your book.

A similar site to check out is LibraryThing.com.

Personal Appearances

If you want people to read your book(s), you will need to get out there and talk about it! Public speaking isn't for everyone, and it's downright scary to most. If public speaking makes you weak in the knees, start out small. Get yourself in front of a room of five people with a 15-minute speech in hand and go from there. You will eventually get the hang of it. Toastmasters is a great organization for people who want to learn public speaking. Some people have grown from being complete introverts to becoming highly paid public speakers because of the training they received from the Toastmasters organization. Look for a club near you; they are everywhere! Another way of getting your feet wet in the world of public speaking is to simply read your book to others! Keep your reading short, (one chapter) and no longer than ten minutes. Be entertaining! Smile and be animated where appropriate. Be sad, with pauses where appropriate. Bring your book to life with your reading. Practice makes perfect, so use your family as your practice audience.

Hold book signings anywhere you can think of. A group of co-workers who had purchased copies of my book on Amazon all wanted their books signed. I held a lunchtime book signing at work and took photos for my website.

A co-worker donated my book, I Was Born to Be, to the workplace library. I got stopped all the time by people who had read that single copy of my book from the library. This led to more traffic to my website and more social media followers. Yeah, they got my book for free, but I just gained a potential reader for any follow-up books. This gave me the idea to donate my books to local libraries and schools.

Getting on TV or the radio isn't all that difficult. Being in the public relations and broadcast media business for many years, I know firsthand how local TV and radio producers are constantly searching for that "go-to" expert or author to fill time, especially on the weekends and early morning shows. Since I wrote a book about being one of the first female firefighters for the California Department of Forestry, I had a topic that was "newsworthy." Write a press release and send it to the local news media. There are many samples of press releases online. I have an example at the end of this book.

If your book is about a trending subject that is hitting the news, now is the time to tell the media you are an expert with a book on the subject. All news media outlets have a tip-line or email for news tips. Don't be afraid to call or email them. Or, you may be a local author with a fiction novel or children's book, and you have a very interesting "back story." It's worth a try to get some "air time." When Fire Girl was published, I sent a press release to the local regional newspaper. They called me in for an interview, took my photograph, and I made the front page! This newspaper article made it to a very well-known blog called "The Mary Sue" that gets millions of views. When my story hit that blog, my book sales went crazy!

Radio stations have pre-taped Sunday morning community programming. Find out which stations in your town have this programming, and see if you can get yourself booked. Having been a producer of one of these shows, I can tell you I was always scrambling to find someone to interview. When an author approached me, I didn't hesitate to put them on the air. My favorite guest was an author who wrote about UFO sightings and abductions!

Here is a side story that has nothing to do with book publishing but everything to do with how the media works. While fighting a forest fire in Washington, my son happened to have his photo taken by an Associated Press photographer. My son not only made the front page of the local paper where the fire was burning, but his photo was published in the Wall Street Journal. Associated Press photographs and news stories are picked up by any and all media outlets nationwide.

If you can get interviewed or photographed by an Associated Press reporter, you have struck gold!

Since you are going to be making public appearances, get professionally photographed so you can include your head shot on your website and marketing materials. Also, put together a press kit that includes your photo, bio, a card, bookmark, or postcard of your book, and a list of places where your book can be purchased. Your press kit should be available to download from your website, and you will need to have some on hand at your events. Give your press kit to any media that shows up and to the people who hosted, booked, or interviewed you. Research the subject of author press kits to get ideas on how to put one together. Don't forget to give key people, (the person who booked and/or interviewed you) a complimentary autographed copy of your book!

Have plenty of books on hand to sell to customers who show up to your events and get acquainted with the smartphone or tablet credit card readers. Hardly anyone carries cash these days.

Not all of your events will be crowd busters. You will have events where only two or three people show up. That's okay; it happens. Sometimes weather or other circumstances beyond your control will keep people from attending. Just keep plugging away and get yourself out there.

CHAPTER 10
Copyright, Trademarks and Other Useful Info

Once your book has been written, it is now copyrighted by you. However, you can take the extra step and have your book registered with the U.S. Copyright Office. The cost is minimal, and you can do it all online. You will get your official copyright notice in the mail in just a few weeks. If you have a series of books, a brand, or a program that you want to get trademarked, you will need to go through the lengthy trademark process and pay a few hundred dollars for the application. You may also need legal help. I used Legalzoom.com when I registered the trademark Rocket Rosie®. They were very reasonable and did the entire thing.

The Library of Congress

The Library of Congress is the research library that officially serves the United States Congress. It is also the de facto national library of the United States. If you would like your book listed in their vast catalog so that libraries from around the United States can look up your book, you will need a control number. You will then put your assigned control number on your copyright page in the front matter of your book.

This is a quote from their website:

"A Library of Congress catalog control number is a unique identification number that the Library of Congress assigns to the catalog record created for each book in its cataloged collections. Librarians use it to locate a specific Library of Congress catalog record in the national databases and to order catalog cards from the

Library of Congress or from commercial suppliers. The purpose of the Pre-assigned Control Number (PCN) program is to enable the Library of Congress to assign control numbers in advance of publication to those titles that may be added to the Library's collections."

It's very easy to get a control number. Just create an account at: www.loc.gov/publish/pcn. Read the rules and follow all of the guidelines. You will find a list of books that are ineligible for the program, such as books already published, ebooks, religious instructional books, expendable educational materials, textbooks below college level, and a few more.

Here are the directions from the Library of Congress:

"Please note that this is a two-step process. All publishers wanting to participate in the PCN Program must first complete and submit an Application to Participate. When the application has been approved, an account number and password will be sent to the publisher via email. Then, publishers participating in the program logon to the PCN system and complete a Pre-assigned Control Number Application Form for each title for which a pre-assigned control number is requested. Based on the information provided by the publisher, Library staff pre-assign a control number to each eligible title. Upon receiving the number, the publisher prints it on the back of the title page (i.e., the copyright page) in the following manner:"

Library of Congress Control Number: 2007012345

CHAPTER 11
The Rest of the Story

Book writing and publishing is a vast subject, and it's difficult to get all of the information in one book. I know that the minute I submit this book for publication, technology will change! Like I said at the beginning, Google and even YouTube will be your best sources of information!

There are millions of authors, and millions of books hit the streets daily. We are just little fish swimming in a vast ocean of words. Unless you are a famous rock star, movie star, or the Pope, it's going to be a long journey for you to get your book to a million readers. You will be very lucky if you sell 1,000 books. Authors that make it big spend many years honing their craft. Many of us read a New York Times List best-seller by an "unknown author" and we think, "Wow, this author made it big with this one book?" Nope, not quite. What you don't know is that this "breakout" author wrote many books before this best seller. He or she wrote essays and entered countless contests. He/she wrote articles for news papers, went to college, and may have received a master's degree in journalism, English literature, or creative writing, and yet their work was rejected by publishers and agents a hundred or more times. This so-called "new" author actually isn't so new! Take a look on Wikipedia at author Cheryl Strayed, who wrote the book Wild. I had never heard of this woman before this book. What you find is that she accomplished all of the things I just mentioned above and more before her book Wild hit the big time and was eventually made into a movie.

You may have a great story to tell, but can you write it? Writing takes practice, and while you practice, you will get rejection and hopefully feedback when you submit your work. Take that feedback and rejection and learn from it.

While doing my research, I read story after story of famous authors whose work was rejected 100 or more times before someone finally published their book. What do the books The Color Purple, Jonathan Livingston Seagull, Harry Potter, The Tale of Peter Rabbit, Gone with the Wind, The Diary of Ann Frank, Jaws, Twilight, Valley of the Dolls, The Great Gatsby (and many more) all have in common? Well, besides being best sellers made into movies, THEY WERE ALL REJECTED numerous times! Get this: Roots, the Pulitzer Prize-winning novel by Alex Haley, was rejected 200 times! Yes, you read that right—200 times!

My advice for you is to write, write, write, and then write some more. If you don't want to get rejected, self-publish and see how that goes. You have absolutely nothing to lose. You will get feedback, you will get experience, you will see your book in print, and you will get reviews. Then, you will write another book and get even better with more feedback, experience, and reviews. Don't expect to get famous, but do expect great satisfaction that you have accomplished something fabulous.

A short word on reviews... You are going to get some bad reviews. NO MATTER WHAT! You can write the most heartwarming story about a kid with cancer and his dog, who helped him through the ordeal, and how they overcame their challenges, and so on and so forth. This story would touch the heart of any human on Earth. Everybody loves your story and can relate on some level. Then, you get a review from that one guy who hated every bit of your story and has no qualms in telling you in detail everything that's wrong with your book. That review is more gut-wrenching than your sad story! It's the ONE negative review that will stay in your brain no matter if you get 100 good reviews. I can tell you all day long to ignore the negative review, but we aren't wired that way. Look at the negative review as a way to make your next book better. Address it, fix it, and move on. Everyone is a critic, and some are grumpier than others.

Now, get going and write that book!
I'm dying to read it!

Resources
Myidentifiers.com - Purchase ISBN
Bowkerlink.com - Register your Publishing Company
Loc.gov/publish/pcn/ - Library of Congress Control Number

Print On Demand Self-Publishing Companies (also ebooks)
Kdp.Amazon.com (Amazon)
Blurb.com
Lulu.com (paperback and hardback)
Ingramspark.com (Ingram company)
ebook Companies
Kdp.amazom.com
Smashwords.com
Leanpub.com (formats and sells all files)

Tools and Directories

www.selfpublishauthors.comwritersdigest.com - A wealth of
information for every author who wants to write a book and get
published. They have great articles about defamation and invasion
of privacy. A must read!
the-efa.org - Editorial Freelancers Association. A great place to
find an editor to hire.
agentquery.com- The largest free database of literary agents.
pw.org - A great non-profit resource for poets and writers.
techtoolsforwriters.com - This website has a great self-editing
toolkit.
Literarymarketplace.com - A directory of Literary Agents,
Publishers and Illustration Agents.
ibpa-online.org - Independent Book Publishers Association
quillbot.com/grammar-check – A Free robust online editor.

Blog Hosting
Wordpress.com(free version)
Wordpress.org (paid version)

Blogger.com (free)
Tumblr (Free - this is a hybrid blog/social media site)
Squarespace.com
Triberr.com - (Free blogging community)

I have written five books in the last 10 years. It's been a learning process, and I'm still learning as technology changes with the blink of an eye. What doesn't change is your story. I can't promise that your book will be read by the masses, but I can promise that writing your story, even if it's only read by a few friends, is rewarding. It was for me.

If you have any questions or need further guidance, feel free to reach out to me at jan@janmendoza.com

☐